Do I Tell?

Written by
Rob Waring and **Maurice Jamall**

to break

to kick

to paint

to throw

bird

bottle

child (children)

garbage can

lake

park

seat

stone

ticket

scared

In the story

 Ji-Sung

 Scott

 Mike

 little girl

Ji-Sung is waiting at the bus stop. He is going to the park.
He meets some boys from school, Scott and his friend, Mike.
"Hi, Ji-Sung," says Scott.
Ji-Sung says, "Oh, hi! What are you doing here?" he asks.
"Nothing much," says Mike. "Ji-Sung, where are you going?"

"I'm going to the park," says Ji-Sung.

"Good. We're going there, too," says Scott.

"Oh," says Ji-Sung. He asks, "What's that in your bag, Scott?"

Scott says, "Oh, this? It's paint."

"Paint? What are you going to paint?" asks Ji-Sung.

"Anything," says Scott.

"You're going to paint anything?" asks Ji-Sung. "I don't understand."

"Do you want to see?" asks Scott.

Ji-Sung does not understand, but he says, "Umm . . . , okay."

Scott looks around. Nobody is watching.

"Is it okay?" Scott asks Mike.

"Yeah, nobody's coming," says Mike. "Okay, do it!" he says.

Ji-Sung is thinking, "What are they going to do?"

Scott takes the paint. He paints the picture on the bus stop.
Ji-Sung shouts, "No, stop. Don't do that!"
Mike and Scott are laughing. "It's okay, it's only fun,"
Scott says. "Nobody can see us."
"But . . . ," says Ji-Sung. "It's wrong!"
"I don't care," says Scott. "It's really fun."

Mike says, "Can I try?"
"Okay," says Scott. He gives the paint to Mike.
He paints the same picture, too.
"Ji-Sung, do you want to try?" asks Scott.
"No way! I'm not going to do that!" he replies.
Scott says, "Hey! Quick! Somebody's coming!"

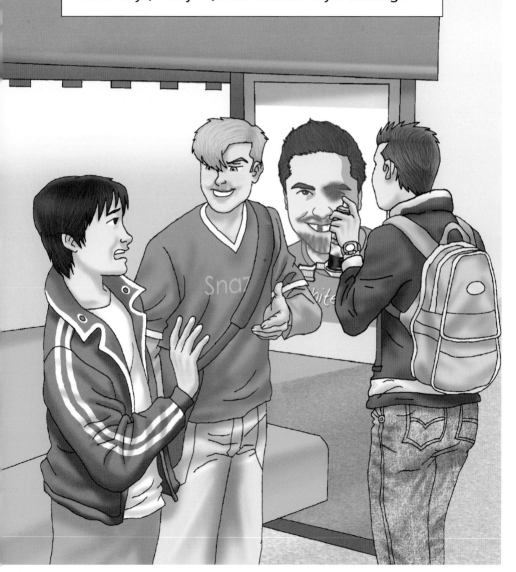

A police officer comes. "What are you boys doing?" asks the police officer.

"Who? Us?" says Scott. "We're waiting for a bus."

The police officer sees the paint. "Did you do this?" he asks Ji-Sung.

Ji-Sung says, "No. No, I didn't." Then the police officer looks at Mike and Scott.

"Did you two boys do this?" he asks Mike and Scott.

"Us? No!" says Scott. "We are *good* boys, officer!" says Mike.

"Be careful, boys," says the police officer. "Don't get into trouble, okay?"
"Of course," they say. "We won't get into trouble."
The police officer leaves. Scott and Mike start laughing.
"He didn't see us," says Mike.
Scott says, "Yeah, he can't do anything about it."
Ji-Sung says nothing. He thinks they are very bad.

Soon, the bus comes. Scott and Mike get on the bus.
Scott says to the bus driver, "One child ticket."
"A child ticket? You can't have a child ticket. How old are you?"
asks the bus driver.
"I'm 10," says Scott.
"No, you're not! You're much older than 10!" says the driver.
"You can't have a child's ticket."

"Okay! Okay!" says Scott. "Here's your money!" He is angry with the bus driver.
Mike is angry, too. He wants to buy a child's ticket, too.
Ji-Sung thinks, "Mike and Scott are very strange. I don't like them very much."
The boys sit down. Everybody looks at them.

Mike and Scott are sitting at the back of the bus. An old woman wants to sit down.
The woman looks at Mike, and says, "Can I sit there?"
Mike answers, "No, because I'm sitting here."
Everybody is very surprised because the old woman cannot sit down. The old woman says nothing. The people on the bus do not like Scott and Mike. They think they are very bad. Ji-Sung thinks so, too.

Ji-Sung gives his seat to the old woman. "You can sit here," he says.

The old woman says, "Thank you! That's very nice of you!"

Ji-Sung watches Mike and Scott. Mike gets a black pen.

"What's he doing?" thinks Ji-Sung.

Mike writes on the back of the seat. Nobody sees him.

Scott smiles at Mike.

Ji-Sung thinks, "Oh no!"

They get off the bus at the park. "Come on, Ji-Sung," says Scott.

Ji-Sung does not like Mike and Scott now. He thinks, "I don't want to be with them. I will get into trouble."

"No, thanks. It's okay," says Ji-Sung to Scott and Mike. "I'm just going home now."

"No. You're not going home. Come with us Ji-Sung. We want to show you a great game," says Scott.

He thinks, "I don't want to go, but Mike and Scott are bigger and stronger than me. I can't say no. What do I do now?"

"Okay, I'm coming," he says. But he does not want to follow them. They walk through the park. Some children are playing.

Suddenly, Mike kicks a garbage can. The garbage goes everywhere. He laughs. Some children look at them. They do not laugh. Then Scott finds some bottles.

"I have an idea," he says to Mike. Scott throws a bottle at another garbage can. The bottle breaks.
"Ha, ha, ha!" laughs Mike.
"I can do better than you," says Mike.
Scott gets some more bottles and gives one to Ji-Sung.
"Here, Ji-Sung, you try!"
"No, thanks," he says.
A little girl is watching him.

Mike throws his bottle and it breaks, too. The boys laugh again.

"This is fun, Mike," says Scott. They both laugh. The boys leave the broken bottles and they walk away. Ji-Sung is very sad. He is worried about Mike and Scott. He puts his bottle in the garbage can.

He thinks, "That was dangerous! It's wrong to do that. I don't want to be with them. I must tell the police, or I may get into trouble. I'm going home!"

Ji-Sung says to Mike and Scott, "Umm . . . , I'm going now."
"No, you're not!" says Scott. "I want to show you our new
game. You'll like it!" he says.
Ji-Sung does not want to be with the boys. But he cannot say
no to Mike and Scott. He is scared of them.
"Come with us," says Scott. Ji-Sung goes with them.

The boys walk to the lake. Mike gives some small stones to Scott and Ji-Sung.

"Are you ready?" asks Scott.

Mike says excitedly, "Come on, Ji-Sung. You take some."

"What are you going to do?" asks Ji-Sung. He is worried about Mike's plan.

Suddenly, Mike and Scott throw the stones at the birds on the lake! Scott's stone nearly hits one of the birds. The birds fly away.

"What are you doing? Don't do that!" says Ji-Sung.

"It's okay, Ji-Sung," says Scott. "It's fun! Let's do it again."

Mike says, "You try, Ji-Sung."

Ji-Sung does not like Mike and Scott. He thinks they are very bad. He wants to tell the police. But he thinks Scott and Mike will be angry with him. He wants to run away. "What do I do?" he thinks. "Do I tell? Or do I say nothing? Scott and Mike are big and strong. Maybe they will hit me!" he thinks.

Ji-Sung thinks, "Oh, what do I do? Do I tell the police?" He feels very bad.

Soon, the girl comes back with a police officer. She tells the police officer about the garbage can, the bottles, and the birds. Mike and Scott cannot see the police officer. They are laughing at the birds. The police officer comes up to the boys.

"They are the bad boys," says the girl to the police officer.
The police officer says, "You three boys will come with me!"
"But I didn't do those things," says Ji-Sung.
"Is that right?" the police officer asks the little girl. "Did he
do those things?"
"I . . . I . . . don't know," says the little girl. "I didn't see.
But he was with the other boys."

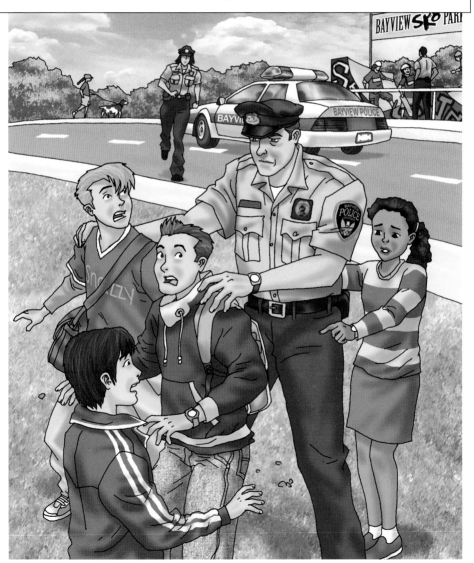

"But I didn't do those things," says Ji-Sung.
"Maybe," says another police officer. "But you were
with these other boys. And you didn't stop them.
You didn't call the police. You're coming with us to
the police station."
"Wait. Please listen," says Ji-Sung. "I'm sorry."
"Not now," says the police officer. "We'll ask your
parents to come to the police station. You can tell us
about it then."
"Oh no," thinks Ji-Sung. "What do I do, now?"